THROUGH THE GLASS WINDOW SHINES THE SUN

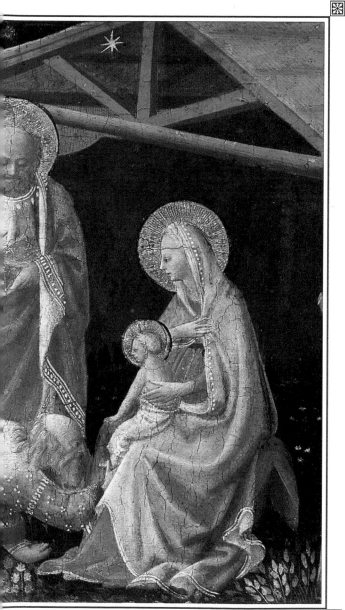

Through the Glass Window Shines the Sun

An Anthology of Medieval Poetry and Prose

Edited by Pamela Norris

THE ADORATION OF THE KINGS, Follower of Fra Angelico

A Bulfinch Press Book
LITTLE, BROWN AND COMPANY
Boston · New York · Toronto · London

FOR ANN, WITH LOVE AND FRIENDSHIP

Text and compilation copyright © 1995 by Pamela Norris

First edition

ISBN 0-8212-2206-6

A CIP catalogue record for this book
is available from the British Library
Library of Congress Catalog Card Number 95-76703

Decorative illustrations by Nadine Wickenden
Designed by David Fordham
Filmset by SX Composing Ltd, Rayleigh, Essex
Please see pages 119-120 for further acknowledgements.

Printed simultaneously in the United States of America by Bulfinch Press,
an imprint and trademark of Little, Brown and Company (Inc.),
in Great Britain by Little, Brown and Company (UK) Ltd,
and in Canada by Little, Brown & Company (Canada) Limited

PRINTED IN ITALY

CONTENTS

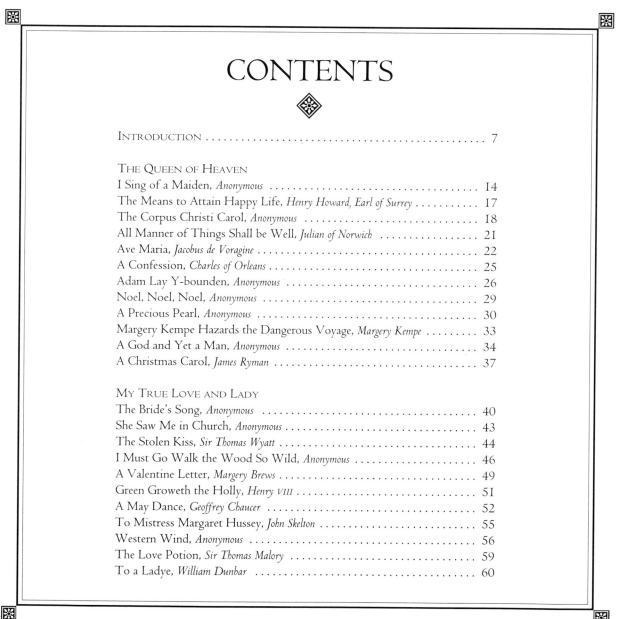

INTRODUCTION

The silver is white, red is the gold;
The robes they lay in fold.
The bailey beareth the bell away;
The lily, the rose, the rose I lay.

Through the Glass Window Shines the Sun brings together writing and painting from across the spectrum of medieval life, spanning a period of around 350 years, from the late twelfth century to the reign of Henry VIII. Many of the texts have been carefully preserved in substantial manuscript collections, but some are mere fragments, rescued perhaps from a fire or a mildewed heap of papers, or consist of a scrappy verse or two scribbled on the back of a more formal document. In most instances we can only guess at the status and identity of the writer – perhaps a cloistered monk, or a travelling singer with sufficient clerkly skills to jot down his repertoire. Even in the case of known writers, biographical details are frequently scarce, and we are left to piece together the life and personality from the works that have survived. Similarly, little is known about many of the artists who produced the magnificent illuminated manuscripts of the period – we may recognize a style, an identifying visual quirk, but the individual artist's history may never fully be known. In such an absence of factual information, texts and visual images become all the more important as clues both to their makers and to the world view that they represent.

It is clear that religious belief was central to every endeavour of medieval life. In peace and in war, whether people earned their bread by spinning yarn or tilling the soil, fighting in the King's service or negotiating the treacherous waters of diplomacy, Christ's life and teaching, interpreted through the dogma and ritual of the church, were the essential reference points. As the poem 'Adam Lay Y-bounden' makes clear, that first fatal bite of the apple in the Garden of Eden laid the basis for centuries of Christian thought. With Adam fell all humanity, only to be redeemed by Christ's Passion on the cross at Calvary.

Had not the apple taken been, the apple taken been,
Never would our Lady have been Heaven's queen.

Out of this simple equation developed a whole schema of sin and redemption, with Christ's mother, the Virgin Mary, as the beloved and compassionate intermediary between human fallibility and the implacable judgement of God.

In the words and images included in THE QUEEN OF HEAVEN, the Christian story is revealed in all its majesty and complexity. The story 'Ave Maria', from Jacobus de Voragine's *Golden Legend*, recalls the momentous greeting of the angel to the young Mary, announcing the miraculous birth of Christ. 'I Sing of a Maiden' also tells of the moment of the incarnation, imagined as the falling of April dew on the grass, here illustrated by Hans Memlinc's tender image of the Virgin with her baby, while 'A Christmas Carol' celebrates the Christmas story, the astonished shepherds and the exotic kings bearing gifts of gold, frankincense and myrrh. The symbolic meaning of 'The Corpus Christi Carol', a haunting narrative of a falcon, a dying knight and a weeping maiden, is revealed in Rogier van der Weyden's painting, 'The Descent from the Cross': Mary's anguish over her crucified son.

The problem of how to live a truly Christian life, often in the face of serious calamity — the devastations of wars and plagues, and the twin scourges of famine and poverty — interested writers as diverse as the reclusive mystic, Julian of Norwich, and the courtier poet, Henry Howard, Earl of Surrey. Julian's famous meditation, 'All Manner of Things Shall be Well', has a modern resonance with its recommendation of positive thinking, while Surrey's programme for a happy life seems similarly up-to-date. The French poet, Charles of Orleans, takes a rather different tack. Captured at Agincourt when he was twenty-one, and held a prisoner in England for twenty-five years, Charles had leisure in which to dream up ways of circumventing religious authority. In his witty poem, 'A Confession', he admits that he has sinned by stealing a kiss, but argues that in order to receive absolution he must restore the stolen object — and therefore kiss again.

Love was a favourite theme of poets and writers, despite the church's strict rules about sexual behaviour. The painting that opens MY TRUE LOVE AND LADY, Lucas Cranach's comic-strip narrative of the events in the Garden of Eden, reminds us that sexual love in the Middle Ages was the great taboo and could lead to dire penalties. At the same time, it was enormously seductive, as the same artist so cleverly shows in another painting in this anthology, the magical study of Eve handing Adam the apple. Who could resist such a glossy red apple, such a tempting Eve? In this pivotal moment before human history begins, we glimpse the Paradise that they – and we – are about to lose for ever: the lion still cohabits peacefully with the lamb, bird and beast feed together in harmony, while the cunning serpent, avatar of Satan, lurks, barely perceptible, in the luxuriant foliage above their heads.

The characteristically cruel or cold lady who features in so much medieval literature was an inheritance from the courtly love tradition of the French troubadour poets, where the young lover worshipped hopelessly from afar. 'I Must Go Walk the Wood So Wild' and the Scottish poet William Dunbar's 'To a Ladye' cast their evidently male speakers in the role of rejected – and bitter – lovers. Dunbar looks in vain in his lady's well-stocked garden for any sign of the humble plant rue, symbol of pity and sympathy: 'Yet leaf nor flower find could I none of Rue.'

Other, perhaps more authentic, voices make themselves heard in this section. Margery Brews' Valentine letter to John Paston expresses the difficulty of finalizing a marriage contract for a young woman without an adequate dowry. 'The Bride's Song', an extract from a longer poem, is also written from the woman's point of view, in this case a very young girl, whose description of her wedding preparations ends with a note of foreboding, 'How should I love, and I so young?' She chooses as her bridal flowers the lily and the rose, the Virgin's flower and the symbol of love, which are constantly referred to in the art and writing of the period. 'Western Wind', an exquisite short poem which was written down with its own stave of accompanying music, movingly conveys the anguish of absence – a sailor perhaps, becalmed on a seemingly endless ocean, praying for the trade winds that will take him home to his loved one.

Two of the great storytellers of the period, Geoffrey Chaucer and Sir Thomas Malory, present many different images of love. Chaucer's *Canterbury Tales*, the stories told by a group of pilgrims on their way to Canterbury to visit the tomb of the martyred Thomas à Becket, include love affairs that range from high romance to slapstick bawdy. In 'A May Dance' the abundant flowers and foliage of a glorious spring day are contrasted with the sterility of unconfessed love, 'never dared he tell her of his grievance'. 'The Love Potion' from Malory's *Le Morte D'Arthur* relates the doomed passion of Tristram and La Belle Isoud. The couple seated at an empty chessboard fittingly express the hopelessness of blighted love.

The diversity of medieval life is suggested by the extracts and poems of IN PEACE, IN WAR. Both Sir Thomas Wyatt and the Earl of Surrey experienced at first hand the perils of serving Henry VIII. Surrey's anguished imprisonment at Windsor, prior to his execution on a trumped-up charge of treason when he was barely thirty years old, is recorded in 'So Cruel Prison'. Wyatt also died young, his diplomatic career tarnished by his association with the discredited Anne Boleyn and the fall of his mentor Cromwell. 'The Perils of Diplomacy' uses the metaphor of a ship steering through stormy seas to describe his hazardous position at the Tudor court.

My galley charged with forgetfulness,
Through sharp seas in winter nights doth pass
'Tween rock and rock; and still my foe, alas,
That is my lord, steereth with cruelness;

Highly gifted and innovative, these poets span the late medieval period and the early Renaissance, speaking at times with startlingly modern voices.

The disputes of kings could be perilous, too, for the common man, requiring service in the army, frequently across the Channel. Henry V's decisive victory at Agincourt in 1415, when English longbowmen defeated a French force that was far superior in numbers, is celebrated in 'Deo Gracias, Anglia' and 'A Song for St George'. In contrast to the polished verse of Wyatt and Surrey, the words are refreshingly simple and direct, with a naturalness of speech that is characteristic of popular songs:

Our king went forth to Normandy
With grace and might of chivalry;
There God for him wrought marvellously,
Wherefore England may call and cry,
'Deo gracias.'

When not fighting, the majority of the population were occupied with some form of production, mainly of food and household goods, and the calendar poem, 'By This Fire I Warm My Hands', celebrates the tasks of the agricultural year. The manuscript of this poem is amusingly illustrated with crude line drawings for each month: a spade for February, a bird on a twig for May, and a very large glass of red wine for Christmas. Calendar miniatures of a far higher quality appear in a number of manuscripts, and are represented in this book by illuminations that include the magnificent *Très Riches Heures* of the Duc de Berry (January, April and May), an April scene with a charming courting couple from an early-sixteenth-century Flemish calendar (page 42), and Simon Bening's evocative October landscape, with its horse-drawn ploughs, the birds swooping to snatch the seed as soon as it is sown, and the woodsmen knocking down acorns for the pigs (page 84).

In an age when life was brief and often brutal, when illiteracy was the norm, and people lived close to nature and to God, miracles, wonders, and MARVELLOUS TALES found a ready audience. Sir John Mandeville's account of his travels is an enchanting collage of the exotic and the ludicrous, though whether he ever left his armchair or even existed is a matter of debate. 'Seth and the Oil of Mercy' gathers together legends of the history of the True Cross, while 'Gatholonabes' Earthly Paradise' tells the story of a thoroughly secular ruler. The thirteenth-century *Golden Legend*, written in Latin and later published in English by William Caxton, was a famous collection of lives of the saints, whose often lurid careers were favourite themes for artists.

Women feature in many stories and not always as saints. 'When Nettles in Winter Bring Forth Roses Red' demonstrates the misogyny that was typical of much medieval writing, as does the ironic 'Of All Creatures Women be Best' in an earlier section, with its contradictory Latin tag. Some commentators equate the enigmatic 'Maiden in the Moor' with the Virgin Mary. She could, however, equally have been a wanton, and here she is matched with the Magdalen, the repentant voluptuary of early church teaching. The 'fair Emilia' in Chaucer's 'Knight's Tale' represents the more socially acceptable face of womanhood, as does the 'Maid of Astolat', who falls in love with the peerless knight Launcelot and dies, leaving a pathetic farewell note.

That favourite medieval pursuit, the hunt, is the subject of two very different narratives. Little is known about either the French poet Marie de France, or the anonymous author of the marvellous allegorical poem *Sir Gawayn and the Grene Knyght*. 'The Wounded Hind' is a prose translation from Marie's lay 'Guigemar', and sets the scene for a love story that is fraught with pain and difficulty before a satisfyingly happy ending. It is illustrated with the white hart from the exterior of the beautiful Wilton Diptych, a mysterious panel composition painted for Richard II. In 1393 Richard had been given a white hart which he kept in Windsor Forest, so the hart may have been painted from life. 'Up Before Dawn' from the *Gawayn* poem describes the early morning preparations for a day's hunting.

It is impossible in a brief introduction to do justice to the richness, diversity and interest of the medieval writers and painters included in this anthology. Readers who would like to explore further will find more information in the final sections of this book. But perhaps in the end it is best to let the works speak for themselves. By just turning the pages, that not-so-distant past is brought into vivid focus in the words and images of the people who lived in Europe in the Middle Ages.

> The stately seats, the ladies bright of hue,
> The dances short, long tales of great delight.

PAMELA NORRIS, 1995

Noel, Noel, Noel,
Sing we with Mirth

THE VIRGIN AND CHILD WITH SAINTS AND DONOR, Gerard David

I SING OF A MAIDEN

I sing of a maiden
That is matchless:
King of all kings
To be her son she chose.

He came also still
Where his mother was,
As dew in April
That falleth on the grass.

He came also still
To his mother's bower,
As dew in April
That falleth on the flower.

He came also still
Where his mother lay,
As dew in April
That falleth on the spray.

Mother and maiden
Was never none but she:
Well may such a lady
God's mother be.

ANONYMOUS

also = as

THE VIRGIN AND CHILD, Hans Memlinc and Workshop

ST BARBARA, The Master of Flemalle

THE MEANS TO ATTAIN HAPPY LIFE

Martial, the things that do attain
The happy life be these, I find:
The riches left, not got with pain;
The fruitful ground; the quiet mind;
The equal friend, no grudge, no strife;
No charge of rule, nor governance;
Without disease the healthful life;
The household of continuance;
The mean diet, no delicate fare;
True wisdom joined with simpleness;
The night discharged of all care,
Where wine the wit may not oppress;
The faithful wife, without debate;
Such sleeps as may beguile the night;
Contented with thine own estate;
Nor wish for death, nor fear his might.

HENRY HOWARD, EARL OF SURREY

THE CORPUS CHRISTI CAROL

Lully, lulley; lully, lulley;
The falcon hath born my mak away.

He bore him up, he bore him down;
He bore him into an orchard brown.

In that orchard there was a hall,
That was hanged with purple and pall.

And in that hall there was a bed;
It was hanged with gold so red.

And in that bed there lieth a knight,
His wounds bleeding day and night.

By that bed's side there kneeleth a may,
And she weepeth both night and day.

And by that bed's side there standeth a stone,
'Corpus Christi' written thereon.

ANONYMOUS

Corpus Christi = the body of Christ   pall = rich brocade
mak = mate   may = maiden

THE DESCENT FROM THE CROSS, Rogier van der Weyden

FLEMISH LANDSCAPE, from the *Histoire Universelle*, attrib. Marmion

ALL MANNER OF THINGS SHALL BE WELL

On one occasion our good Lord said, 'All things shall be well', and another time He said, 'Thou shalt see for thyself that all manner of things shall be well'; and in these two sayings the soul understood several things. One was this: that He wants us to know that not only does He pay attention to noble and great matters, but also to little and to small: to low and to simple, to one and to other, and this is what He means when He says, 'All manner of things shall be well', for He wants us to know that the least matter will not be forgotten. Another meaning is this: that evil deeds are done in our sight and such great suffering endured that it seems impossible to us that it should ever come to a good conclusion; and we look upon all this, sorrowing and mourning for it, so that we cannot rest in the blissful beholding of God as we should do. And the cause is this: that the use of our reason is now so blind, so low and so simple, that we cannot know that sublime, marvellous wisdom, the might and goodness of the blissful Trinity. And this is what He means when He says, 'Thou shalt see thyself that all manner of things shall be well', as if He were saying, 'Pay attention now, faithfully and trustfully, and at the final moment thou shalt verily see it in the fullness of joy.' And thus in these same five words aforesaid, 'I may make all things well', I take a mighty comfort from all the works of our Lord God that are still to come.

From JULIAN OF NORWICH, *Revelations of Divine Love*

AVE MARIA

Of the salutation that the angel brought to the glorious Virgin, we read an example of a noble knight who to amend his life gave and rendered himself into an abbey of Citeaux, and, forasmuch as he was no clerk, there was assigned to him a master to teach him, and to be with the brethren clerks, but he could learn nothing in the long time that he was there save these two words: 'Ave Maria', which words he had so sore imprinted in his heart that always he had them in his mouth wheresoever he was.

At last he died and was buried in the churchyard of the brethren. It happened after, that upon the grave grew a marvellously beautiful fleur-de-lis, and in every flower was written in letters of gold: 'Ave Maria'. All the brethren marvelled at this miracle, and they opened the tomb, and found that the root of this fleur-de-lis came out of the mouth of the said knight, and anon they understood that our Lord would have him honoured for the great devotion that he had to say these words: 'Ave Maria'.

From JACOBUS DE VORAGINE, *The Golden Legend*

Ave Maria = Hail Mary, the words spoken to
Mary by the angel, announcing the miraculous
birth of Christ

ALTARPIECE: THE ANNUNCIATION, Follower of Fra Angelico

JOHN, DUKE OF BEDFORD, AT PRAYER BEFORE ST GEORGE, The Bedford Hours, The Master of the Munich Golden Legend

A CONFESSION

My ghostly father, I me confess,
First to God and then to you,
That at a window – you know how –
I stole a kiss of great sweetness;
The doing was spontaneous,
But it is done, not undone, now.

My ghostly father, I me confess,
First to God and then to you.
But I restore it shall doubtless
Again, if so be that I can;
And that, God, I make a vow,
And else I ask forgiveness.

My ghostly father, I me confess,
First to God and then to you.

CHARLES OF ORLEANS

ghostly = spiritual

ADAM LAY Y-BOUNDEN

Adam lay y-bounden, bounden in a bond,
Four thousand winters thought he not too long.

And all was for an apple, an apple that he took,
As learned men find written in their Book.

Had not the apple taken been, the apple taken been,
Never would our Lady have been Heaven's queen.

Blessed be the time that apple taken was,
Therefore we may sing, 'Deo gracias.'

ANONYMOUS

y-bounden = tied up (by bonds, or ropes)
Book = Bible
Deo gracias = Thanks be to God

ADAM AND EVE (detail), Lucas Cranach the Elder

THE VISITATION, The Hours of Marshal Jean de Boucicaut

NOEL, NOEL, NOEL

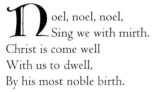 oel, noel, noel,
  Sing we with mirth.
Christ is come well
With us to dwell,
By his most noble birth.

Under a tree
When sporting me
Alone by a wood-side,
I heard a maid
That sweetly said,
'I am with child this tide.' *Noel, etc*

'Graciously
Conceived have I
The Son of God so sweet;
His gracious will
I put me till,
As mother him to keep.' *Noel, etc*

'Both night and day
I will him pray,
And hear his laws taught,
And every dell
His true gospel
In his apostles fraught.' *Noel, etc*

'This ghostly case
Doth me embrace,
Without despite or mock;
With my darling,
"Lullay" to sing,
And lovely him to rock.' *Noel, etc*

'Without distress
In great lightness
I am both night and day.
This heavenly fod
In his childhood
Shall daily with me play.' *Noel, etc*

'Soon must I sing
With rejoicing,
For the time is all run
That I shall child,
All undefiled,
The King of Heaven's Son.' *Noel, etc*

ANONYMOUS

this tide = at this time
every dell = entirely
fraught = entrusted

✠

ghostly case = spiritual task
fod = child
(to) child = to give birth

A PRECIOUS PEARL

Pearls inlaid of royal price
 There men might by grace have seen,
When she, as fresh as fleur-de-lis,
Down the slope did swiftly turn.
Blazing white was her robe of fine linen,
Slashed at the sides, and wonderfully wrought
With the purest pearls, in my opinion,
That ever yet have charmed my sight;
Her hanging sleeves, as I observed them,
With double pearls were arrayed about,
And her dazzling gown was decorated
With precious pearls on its fabric light.

An ornate crown also wore that girl,
Of marjories and no other gem,
High pinnacled in clear white pearl,
With figured flowers on perfect stem.
On her brow she bore no ornament more,
Save only the veil which wrapped her round;
Her face was as grave as duke or earl,
Her white skin purer than white whale's bone.
Like shining gold her fair hair shone,
Lying unbound on her shoulders light,
Her perfect pallor yet wanted none
Of precious pearl in border bright.

She was decked at wrist and also at hem,
At hands, at sides, at bodice-rim,
With milk-white pearls and no other gem,
And burnished white was all her gown.
But a wondrous pearl without a flaw
Was set so firm upon her breast,
A man would doubt he could be sure
How best its worth he might assess.
I think no tongue could find the power
Truly to talk about that sight,
So fresh it was, so clear and pure,
That precious pearl there glowing white.

From ANONYMOUS, *Pearl*

marjories = pearls

30

ST DOROTHY (detail), The Master of the St Bartholomew Altarpiece

THE EXIT FROM THE ARK, The Bedford Hours, The Master of the Munich Golden Legend

MARGERY KEMPE HAZARDS THE DANGEROUS VOYAGE ACROSS THE SEA

On the next day, bright and early, there came to this woman the good priest, who was like a son to her, and he said, 'Mother, excellent tidings! We have a favourable wind, thanks be to God.' And at once she gave praise to our Lord, and prayed Him of His mercy to grant them a continuation of the good wind and weather, so that they might return home in safety. And it was answered and ordained in her soul that they should go their way in Jesus's name.

When the priest knew that she intended, whatever happened, to make the journey, he said, 'Mother, there is no ship – only a small vessel.'

She replied, 'Son, God is as mighty in a little ship as in a great one, so I will go on board with God's permission.'

When they were in the little ship, there arose great tempests and stormy weather. Then they cried to God for grace and mercy, and presently the tempests ceased and they had fair weather, and sailed all through the night and the next day until it was evensong-time, and then they reached dry land. And when they were on shore, the aforesaid woman fell down on her knees, kissing the ground, and greatly thanking God who had brought them home in safety.

From *The Book of Margery Kempe*, 1436

A GOD AND YET A MAN

A god and yet a man?
A maid and yet a mother?
Wit wonders what wit can
Conceive this or the other?

A god and can he die?
A dead man, can he live?
What wit can well reply?
What reason reason give?

God, truth itself, doth teach it;
Man's wit sinks too far under
By reason's power to reach it:
Believe and cease to wonder.

ANONYMOUS

CHRIST MOCKED (THE CROWNING WITH THORNS), Hieronymus Bosch

THE APPARITION OF THE ANGELS TO THE SHEPHERDS, The Book of Hours of René Anjou, The Egerton Master

A CHRISTMAS CAROL

Gloria in altissimis,
    For now is born the King of Bliss.

When Christ was born, an angel bright
To shepherds keeping sheep that night
Came and said with heavenly light,
    'Now Christ is born, the King of Bliss.'

They felt great dread of that same light
That shone so bright that time of night
Through the virtue, the grace, and might
    Of God's son, the King of Bliss.

The angel said, 'Dread you nothing;
Behold, to you great joy I bring,
And unto all that be living,
    For now is born the King of Bliss.

'Go to Bethlehem, and there you shall
With Mary mild in an ox stall
Find an infant that men shall call
    The Son of God and King of Bliss.'

They went forth to Bethlehem that stound,
And, as he told, a child they found
In an ox stall in rags wound,
    The Son of God and King of Bliss.

The shepherds then went home again,
Magnifying God, in certain,
In all that they had heard and seen
    Of God's son, the King of Bliss.

On Twelfth Day came kings three
With gold, incense, and myrrh so free,
Unto Bethlehem to seek and see
    The Son of God and King of Bliss.

In terra pax hominibus

JAMES RYMAN

Gloria in altissimis = Gloria in the highest
stound = time
In terra pax hominibus = Peace on earth to humankind

-My- Grue Love and Lady

WHO HATH MY HEART TRULY,
BE SURE, AND EVER SHALL

ADAM AND EVE IN THE GARDEN OF EDEN, Lucas Cranach the Elder

THE BRIDE'S SONG

The maidens came
When I was in my mother's bower:
I had all that I would.
The bailey beareth the bell away;
The lily, the rose, the rose I lay.

The silver is white, red is the gold;
The robes they lay in fold.
The bailey beareth the bell away;
The lily, the rose, the rose I lay.

And through the glass window shines the sun.
How should I love, and I so young?
The bailey beareth the bell away;
The lily, the rose, the rose I lay.

ANONYMOUS

PORTRAIT OF A LADY, Workshop of Rogier van der Weyden

LOVERS IN A GARDEN, April scene from a Flemish calendar

SHE SAW ME IN CHURCH

Go, little bill, and commend me heartily
Unto her that I call my true love and lady,
By this same true tokening,
That she saw me in church one Friday in the morning,
With a sparrow-hawk on my hand,
And my companion did by her stand,
And an old woman sat her by,
Who little knew of courtesy;
And often at her she did smile
To look at me for a while.

And yet by this, another token,
To the church she came with a gentlewoman,
And just behind the church door
They knelt together on the floor,
And fast they did pitter-patter —
I hope they said matins together.
Yet once or twice, at the very least,
She did on me her eyes cast.
Then I went out privately
And greeted them both most courteously.

By all these tokens, truly,
Commend me to her heartily.   ANONYMOUS

bill = note

THE STOLEN KISS

To his love whom he has kissed against her will

Alas, Madam, for stealing of a kiss,
Have I so much your mind therein offended?
Or have I done so grievously amiss
That by no means it may not be amended?
Revenge you then; the readiest way is this:
Another kiss my life it shall have ended.
For, to my mouth the first my heart did suck,
The next shall clean out of my breast it pluck.

Sir Thomas Wyatt

CHARLEMAGNE AND THE MEETING OF SAINTS JOACHIM AND ANNE, The Master of Moulins (Jean Hey)

I MUST GO WALK THE WOOD SO WILD

I must go walk the wood so wild
And wander here and there
In dread and deadly fear,
For where I trusted I am beguiled,
And all for one.

Thus am I banished from my bliss
By craft and false pretence,
Faultless, without offence,
As of return no surety is,
And all for fear of one.

My bed shall be under the greenwood tree,
A tuft of brakes under my head,
As one from joy were fled.
Thus from my life day by day I flee,
And all for one.

The running streams shall be my drink,
Acorns shall be my food;
Nothing may do me good,
But when of your beauty I do think,
And all for love of one.

ANONYMOUS

✠

THE LOVER ASLEEP, RISING, AND GOING FOR A WALK, *Roman de la Rose*, The Master of the Prayer Books of *c.* 1500

CHRISTINE DE PISAN, WRITING, from *The Collected Works of Christine de Pisan*, The Master of the Cité des Dames

A VALENTINE LETTER

Unto my right well-beloved Valentine, John Paston, Squire, be this note delivered

Right reverend and worshipful and my right well-beloved Valentine, I commend myself to you very heartily, desiring to hear of your wellbeing, which I beseech Almighty God long for to preserve to His pleasure and your heart's desire. And if it pleases you to hear of my welfare, I am not in good health of body or of heart, nor shall I be until I hear from you. For there knows no creature what pain I endure, and for my life I dare not it discover.

My lady mother has laboured the matter [the marriage settlement] to my father very diligently, but she is unable to get more than you already know about, for which, God knows, I am most sorry. But if you love me, as I trust in truth you do, you will not leave me because of this. For even if you did not have half the livelihood that you possess, if it meant working as hard as any woman living, I would not forsake you. And if you command me to keep myself faithful wherever I go, indeed I will do everything in my power to love you and only you. If my friends say that I am making a mistake, they still won't prevent me from doing this. My heart bids me evermore to love you truly above all earthly thing. However angry people may be now, I trust things will be better in the future.

No more to you at this time, but the Holy Trinity keep you safe. And I beseech you that this note is seen by no other creature on earth except for yourself.

This letter was composed at Topcroft with a very heavy heart.

By your own M. B.

Margery Brews, to John Paston Esq., February 1477

✠

HENRY VIII SEATED, READING IN A BEDROOM, from John Mallard's psalter

GREEN GROWETH THE HOLLY

Green groweth the holly,
　So doth the ivy.
Though winter blasts blow never so high,
Green groweth the holly.

As the holly groweth green
And never changeth hue,
So am I, ever hath been,
Unto my lady true.

As the holly groweth green
With ivy all alone,
When flowers cannot be seen,
And greenwood leaves be gone.

Now unto my lady
Promise to her I make,
From all other only
To her I me betake.

Adieu, mine own lady,
Adieu, my special,
Who hath my heart truly,
Be sure, and ever shall.

The King, HENRY VIII

A MAY DANCE

The neglected wife, Dorigen, is desired by the handsome squire, Aurelius

So on a day, right in the morrow-tide,
Unto a garden that was there beside . . .
They went and played them all the long day.
And this was on the sixth morning of May,
Which May had painted with his soft showers
This garden full of leaves and of flowers;
And craft of man's hand so curiously
Arrayed had this garden, truly,
That never was there garden of such price,
But if it were the very Paradise.
The odour of flowers and the fresh sight
Would have made any heart feel light
That ever was born, unless great sickness,
Or great sorrow held it in distress;
So full it was of beauty with pleasance.
After dinner went they to dance
And sing also, save Dorigen alone,
Who made always her complaint and her moan
Because she did not see him on the dance go
Who was her husband and her love also . . .
   Upon this dance, amongst other men,
Danced a squire before Dorigen,
That fresher was and jollier of array,
As to my doom, than is the month of May.
He singeth, danceth, better than any man

That is, or was, since first the world began.
With this he was, if men should him describe,
One of the best-looking men alive:
Young, strong, right virtuous, and rich and wise,
And well beloved, and held in great price.
And in short, if the truth I tell shall,
Unknown to this Dorigen at all,
This lusty squire, servant to Venus,
Who was named Aurelius,
Had loved her best of any creature
Two years and more, such was his adventure,
But never dared he tell her of his grievance:
Without a cup he drank all his penance.
He did despair; nothing dared he say,
Save in his songs somewhat would he betray
His woe, as in a general complaining,
He said he loved, and was beloved nothing.
Of such matter made he many lays,
Songs, complaints, roundels, virelays,
How that he dared not his sorrow tell,
But languished as a fury doth in hell . . .

From Geoffrey Chaucer, 'The Franklin's Tale'

52

GLADNESS LEADS THE DANCE: THE LOVER AND HIS ROSE, *Roman de la Rose,* The Master of the Prayer Books of *c.* 1500

PORTRAIT OF A WOMAN OF THE HOFER FAMILY, Unknown Swabian artist

TO MISTRESS MARGARET HUSSEY

Merry Margaret,
    As midsummer flower,
Gentle as falcon
Or hawk of the tower;

With solace and gladness,
Much mirth and no madness,
All good and no badness,
So joyously,
So maidenly,
So womanly
Her demeaning
In every thing,
Far, far passing
That I can indite,
Or suffice to write
Of merry Margaret,
As midsummer flower,

Gentle as falcon
Or hawk of the tower;

As patient and as still,
And as full of good will,
As fair Isaphill;
Coriander,
Sweet pomander,
Good Cassander;
Steadfast of thought,
Well made, well wrought;
Far may be sought
Erst that ye can find
So courteous, so kind
As merry Margaret,
This midsummer flower,
Gentle as falcon
Or hawk of the tower.

JOHN SKELTON

Isaphill and Cassander = women in classical literature
Gentle as falcon = the female peregrine falcon was famed for her gentle nature

WESTERN WIND

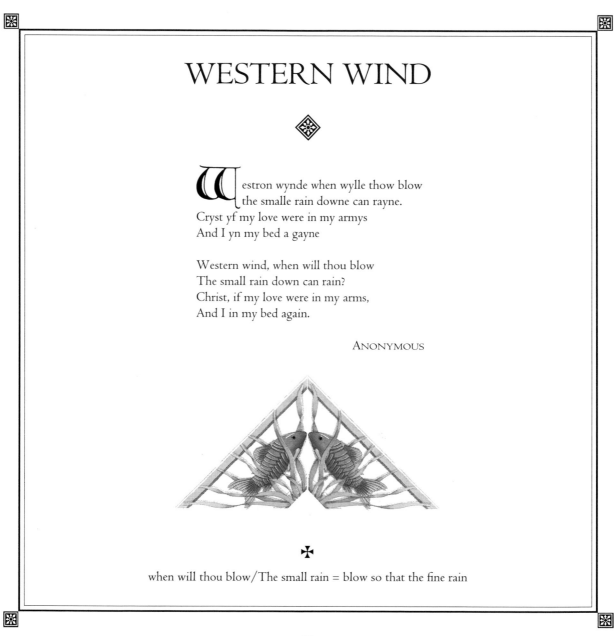

Westron wynde when wylle thow blow
the smalle rain downe can rayne.
Cryst yf my love were in my armys
And I yn my bed a gayne

Western wind, when will thou blow
The small rain down can rain?
Christ, if my love were in my arms,
And I in my bed again.

ANONYMOUS

when will thou blow/The small rain = blow so that the fine rain

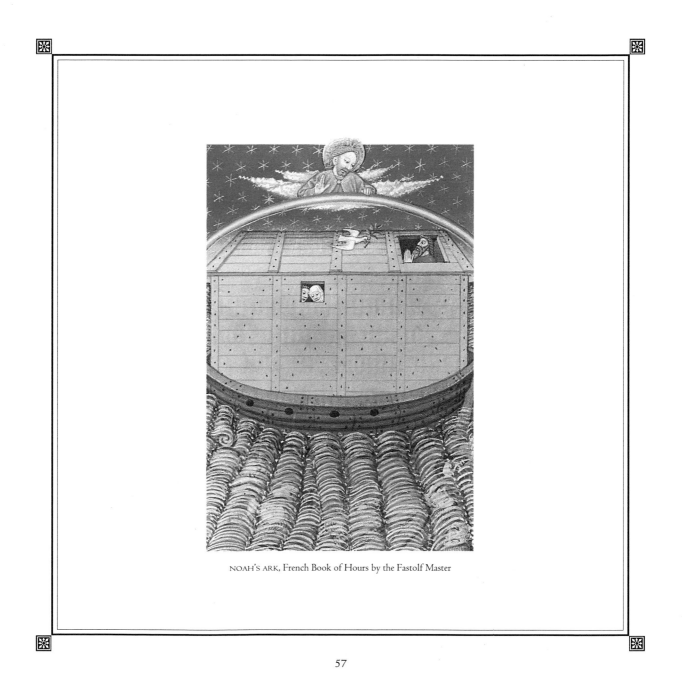

NOAH'S ARK, French Book of Hours by the Fastolf Master

TWO SEATED FIGURES WITH EMPTY CHESSBOARD, from *Historia Alexandri Magni*

THE LOVE POTION

HOW SIR TRISTRAM AND HIS SERVANT GOVERNALE ESCORTED LA BELLE ISOUD TO HER MARRIAGE WITH KING MARK OF CORNWALL, AND OF THE LOVE POTION THAT WENT ASTRAY

So to make a short conclusion, La Belle Isoud was made ready to go with Sir Tristram, and Dame Bragwaine went with her as her chief gentlewoman, with many others. And then the Queen, La Belle Isoud's mother, gave unto Dame Bragwaine, her daughter's gentlewoman, and unto Governale a drink, and charged them that on the day that King Mark should wed, that same day they should give him that drink, so that King Mark should drink unto La Belle Isoud, 'and then I undertake,' said the Queen, 'each shall love the other all the days of their life.' So this drink was given to Governale and to Dame Bragwaine, and then anon Sir Tristram and La Belle Isoud took to sea.

And when they were in their cabin, it happened that they were thirsty, and they saw a little gold flask standing nearby, and it seemed by the colour and taste that it was noble wine. So Sir Tristram took the flask in his hand, and said, 'Madame Isoud, here is the best drink that ever ye drank, which Dame Bragwaine your maid and Governale my servant have kept for themselves.' And then they laughed and made good cheer, and each drank to the other freely, and they thought that no drink that ever they drank to another was so sweet or so good. But as soon as their drink was in their bodies, they loved each other so well, that their love never departed for weal or woe.

And thus happened first the love between Sir Tristram and La Belle Isoud, a love that never left them all the days of their life.

From Sir Thomas Malory, *Le Morte D'Arthur*

TO A LADYE

Sweet Rose of virtue and of gentleness,
Delightsome Lily of every lustiness,
Richest in bounty, and in beauty clear,
And every virtue that is held most dear,
Except, only, that you are merciless.

Into your garden, this day, I did pursue,
There saw I flowers that fresh were of hue;
Both white and red most lusty to be seen,
And wholesome herbs upon stalks green;
Yet leaf nor flower find could I none of Rue.

I doubt that March with his cold blasts so keen
Has slain this gentle herb of which I do complain,
Whose piteous death does to my heart such pain
That I would make to plant his root again,
So comforting his leaves to me have been.

WILLIAM DUNBAR

lustiness = pleasure
lusty = attractive
make = compose, write poetry

COURTLY FIGURES ON HORSEBACK, May scene from *Les Très Riches Heures du Duc de Berry*, The Limbourg Brothers

In Peace, In War

By this Fire I Warm my Hands,
and with my Spade I Delve my Lands

THE PROCESSION TO CALVARY, Pieter Brueghel the Elder

SO CRUEL PRISON

PRISONED IN WINDSOR, HE RECOUNTETH HIS PLEASURES THERE PASSED

So cruel prison how could betide, alas,
    As proud Windsor? where I in lust and joy
With a king's son my childish years did pass
In greater feast than Priam's sons of Troy;

Where each sweet place returns a taste full sour:
The large green courts, where we were wont to
                                            hove,
With eyes cast up unto the maidens' tower,
And easy sighs, such as folk draw in love.

The stately seats, the ladies bright of hue,
The dances short, long tales of great delight,
With words and looks that tigers could but rue,
Where each of us did plead the other's right.

The secret groves which oft we made resound
Of pleasant plaint and of our ladies' praise,
Recording oft what grace each one had found,
What hope of speed, what dread of long delays.

The secret thoughts imparted with such trust,
The wanton talk, the divers change of play,
The friendship sworn, each promise kept so just,
Wherewith we passed the winter night away.

And with this thought the blood forsakes the face,
The tears berain my cheeks of deadly hue;
The which as soon as sobbing sighs, alas,
Upsupped have, thus I my plaint renew:

'O place of bliss, renewer of my woes,
Give me account where is my noble fere,
Whom in thy walls thou doest each night enclose,
To other lief, but unto me most dear.'

Echo, alas, that doth my sorrow rue,
Returns thereto a hollow sound of plaint.
Thus I alone, where all my freedom grew,
In prison pine with bondage and restraint.

And with remembrance of the greater grief
To banish the less, I find my chief relief.

✠

fere = companion
lief = beloved

HENRY HOWARD, EARL OF SURREY

THE TOWER OF LONDON, manuscript of the poems of Charles of Orleans

THE DUC DE BERRY HOSTS A SUMPTUOUS FEAST, January scene from *Les Très Riches Heures du Duc de Berry*, The Limbourg Brothers

BRING US IN GOOD ALE

Bring us in good ale, and bring us in good ale,
For our blessed Lady's sake, bring us in good ale.

Bring us in no brown bread, for that is made of bran,
Nor bring us in no white bread, for therein is no fun,
But bring us in good ale. *Chorus*

Bring us in no beef, for that has many bones,
But bring us in good ale, for that goes down at once,
And bring us in good ale. *Chorus*

Bring us in no bacon, for that is passing fat,
But bring us in good ale, and give us enough of that,
And bring us in good ale. *Chorus*

Bring us in no mutton, for that is often lean,
Nor bring us in no tripes, for they are seldom clean,
But bring us in good ale. *Chorus*

Bring us in no eggs, for they have many shells,
But bring us in good ale, and give us nothing else,
And bring us in good ale. *Chorus*

Bring us in no puddings, for those contain goats' blood,
Nor bring us any venison, for that's not for our good,
But bring us in good ale. *Chorus*

Bring us in no capon's flesh, for that is often dear,
Nor bring us in no ducks' flesh, for they slobber in the mere,
But bring us in good ale. *Chorus*   ANONYMOUS

I HAVE A YOUNG SISTER

I have a young sister
Far beyond the sea;
Many be the love-tokens
That she sent to me.

She sent me the cherry
Without any stone;
And so she did the dove
Without any bone;

She sent me the briar
Without any branch;
She bade me love my sweetheart
Without longing.

How should any cherry
Be without stone?
And how should any dove
Be without bone?

How should any briar
Be without branch?
How should I love my sweetheart
Without longing?

When the cherry was a flower:
Then had it no stone.
When the dove was an egg:
Then had it no bone.

When the briar was a seed:
Then had it no bough.
When the maiden hath that she loveth:
She is without longing.

ANONYMOUS

ST CATHERINE OF ALEXANDRIA (detail), Raphael

GARDEN SCENE, THE LOVER WITHOUT, *Roman de la Rose,* The Master of the Prayer Books of *c.* 1500

IN A GLORIOUS GARDEN GREEN

This day day dawns
   This gentle day day dawns,
This gentle day dawns,
And I must home gone.
This day day dawns,
This gentle day dawns,
And I must home gone.

In a glorious garden green
Saw I sitting a comely queen
Among the flowers that fresh been.
She gathered a flower and sat between.
The lily-white rose me thought I saw,
The lily-white rose me thought I saw,
And ever she sang:

   This day day dawns
   This gentle day dawns,
   This gentle day dawns
   And we must home gone.
   And I must home gone.
   This gentle day dawns,
   This gentle day dawns,
   And we must home gone.

In that garden be flowers of hue,
The sweet gillyflower that she well knew;
The fleur-de-lis that made her rue;
She said, 'The white rose is most true
This garden to rule by rightful law.'
The lily-white rose me thought I saw,
And ever she sang:

   This gentle day dawns
   This gentle day dawns,
   And I must home gone.
   This gentle day dawns,
   This day day dawns,
   This gentle day dawns,
   And we must home gone.

ANONYMOUS

DEO GRACIAS, ANGLIA

Deo gracias, Anglia,
Redde pro victoria.
Give thanks to God, Anglia,
Thanks for victory.

Our king went forth to Normandy
With grace and might of chivalry;
There God for him wrought marvellously,
Wherefore England may call and cry,
'Deo gracias.'

He set a siege, the truth for to say,
To Harfleurs town with royal array;
That town he won and made a fray
That France shall rue until Doomsday.
'Deo gracias.'

Then went our king with all his host
Through France, for all the French's boast;
He spared, no doubt, nor least nor most,
Till he came to Agincourt coast.
'Deo gracias.'

Then, forsooth, that knight comely
In Agincourt field he fought manly;
Through grace of God most mighty
He had both the field and victory.
'Deo gracias.'

There duke and earl, lord and baron,
Were taken and slain, and that well soon,
And some were led into London
With joy and mirth and great renown.
'Deo gracias.'

Now gracious God, may He save our king,
His people and all his well-willing;
Give him a good life and a good ending,
That we with joy may safely sing,
'Deo gracias.'

ANONYMOUS

coast = region
well-willing = those who wish him well

THE CAPTURE OF ANTIOCH, *Storie degli Imperatori*

GEORGE GRISZE, Hans Holbein

THE PERILS OF DIPLOMACY

My galley charged with forgetfulness,
Through sharp seas in winter nights doth pass
'Tween rock and rock; and still my foe, alas,
That is my lord, steereth with cruelness;
And every hour a thought in readiness,
As though that death were light in such a case.
An endless wind doth tear the sails apace
Of forced sighs and trusty fearfulness.
A rain of tears, a cloud of dark disdain,
Have done the wearied cords great hinderance;
Wreathed with error and with ignorance.
The stars be hid that lead me to this pain;
Drowned is reason that should be my comfort,
And I remain, despairing of the port.

SIR THOMAS WYATT

✠

ST GEORGE, French Book of Hours by the Fastolf Master

A SONG FOR ST GEORGE

Enforce we us with all our might
To love Saint George, our Lady's knight.

Worship of virtue is the meed,
And follows him ay of right;
To worship George then have we need,
Which is our sovereign Lady's knight.

He saved the maid from dragon's dread,
And 'fraid all France and put to flight.
At Agincourt – the chronicle ye read –
The French him see foremost in fight.

In his virtue he will us lead
Against the Fiend, the foul wight,
And with his banner us overspread,
If we him love with all our might.

ANONYMOUS

meed = reward
'fraid = frightened
wight = creature

OF ALL CREATURES WOMEN BE BEST

Of all creatures women be best,
Cuius contrarium verum est.

In every place you may well see
That women are true as turtle on tree,
Not free in their language, but speaking secretly,
And great joy among them it is for to be. *Chorus*

The constancy of women will never be done,
So gentle, so courteous, they be every one,
Meek as a lamb, still as a stone,
Crooked or crabbed find you none. *Chorus*

Men are more trouble a thousandfold,
And I wonder how they dare be so bold
Against women for to hold,
Seeing them so patient, soft and cold. *Chorus*

For, tell a women all your counsel,
And she can keep it wonderfully well;
She had rather go quick to hell
Than to her neighbour she would it tell. *Chorus*

Now, say well by women or else be still,
For they never displeased men by their will;
To be angry or wroth they have no skill,
For I believe they think nothing ill. *Chorus*

Think you that women like to chatter,
Or against their husbands they love to clatter?
No – they would fast on bread and water,
Rather than act so in such a matter. *Chorus*

To the tavern they will not go,
Nor to the alehouse, never the more,
For, God knows, it would give them woe
To spend their husbands' money so.

 Of all creatures women be best,
 Cuius contrarium verum est.

ANONYMOUS

Cuius contrarium verum est =
The truth is the opposite of this

turtle = turtle-dove

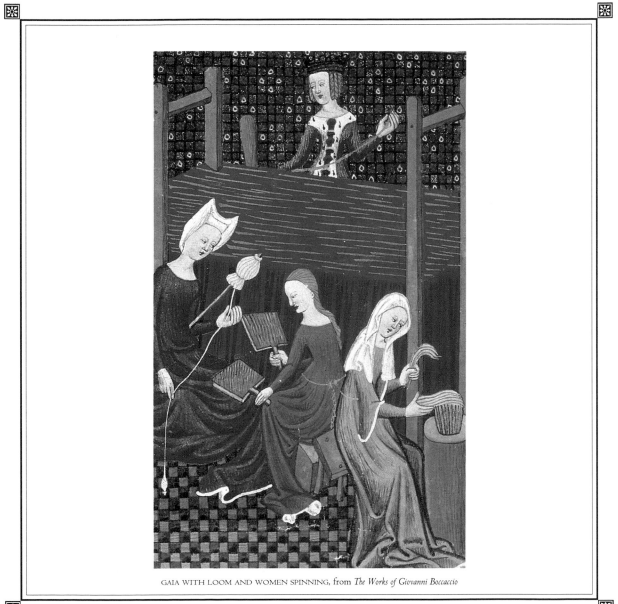

GAIA WITH LOOM AND WOMEN SPINNING, from *The Works of Giovanni Boccaccio*

THE PAYMENT OF JUDAS, The Sforza Hours, Giovan Pietro Birago

A FRIENDSHIP LOST

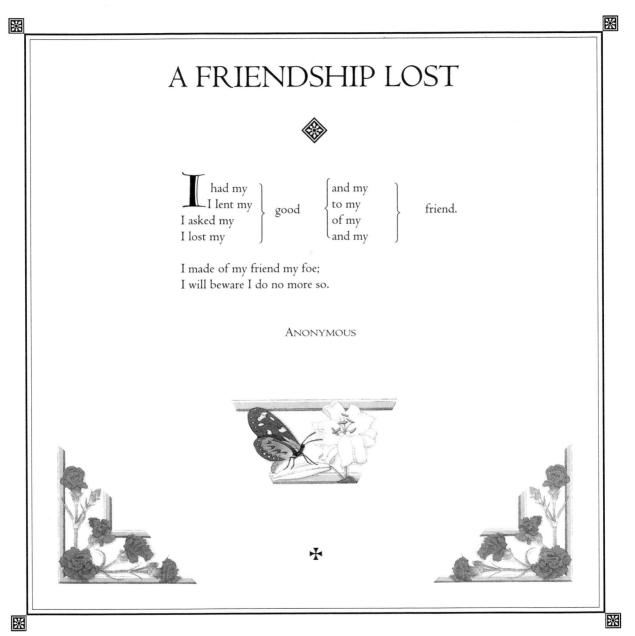

I
had my ⎫ ⎧ and my
I lent my ⎬ good ⎨ to my
I asked my ⎭ ⎩ of my friend.
I lost my ⎭ and my ⎭

I made of my friend my foe;
I will beware I do no more so.

ANONYMOUS

✠

81

A FRUITFUL GARDEN

The garden was, by measuring,
Quite even, a square encompassing;
It was as long as it was broad.
Of fruit had every tree its load,
Except for the odd blighted tree,
Of which there were but two or three.
There were, and that know I full well,
Of pomegranates a great deal,
A fruit that's popular to pick,
And most of all when folk are sick.
Trees there were, in any number,
Whose harvest boughs sweet nutmegs cumber,
Those tiny fruit whose fragrant savour
Gives to food its spicy flavour.
Almonds flourished in great plenty,
Figs, and many a bounteous date-tree.
In abundance grew there every spice,
Clove-gillyflowers and liquorice,
Ginger and Grain of Paradise,

Cinnamon and zedoary of price,
And many another tasty treat
That adds delight to what we eat.
A host of familiar trees there were
That peaches, quinces, apples bear,
Medlars, plums, pears, and sweet chestnuts,
And cherries, always favourites . . .
There sprang the violet, sparkling new,
The fresh periwinkle, rich in hue,
And flowers yellow, white and red,
Such plenty grew there never in mead.
Very gay was all the ground, ornate,
With a powdered look as if from paint,
With many a bright and varied flower
That perfumed the air with a good savour.

From GUILLAUME DE LORRIS, *Roman de la Rose,*
trans. GEOFFREY CHAUCER

Grain of Paradise = cardamom   zedoary = a form of ginger plant, used as a spice and stimulant

AN ORCHARD WITH PEOPLE PICKING FRUIT, from Croissen's *Manual of Agriculture*

OCTOBER: PLOUGHING AND SOWING, Flemish Book of Hours, Simon Bening

BY THIS FIRE I WARM MY HANDS

JANUARY	**B**y this fire I warm my hands,
FEBRUARY	And with my spade I delve my lands.
MARCH	Here I set my seeds to spring,
APRIL	And here I hear the birds sing.
MAY	I am as light as bird on bough,
JUNE	And I weed my corn well enough.
JULY	With my scythe my mead I mow,
AUGUST	And here I shear my corn full low.
SEPTEMBER	With my flail I earn my bread,
OCTOBER	And here I sow my wheat so red.
NOVEMBER	At Martin's mass I kill my swine,
DECEMBER	And at Christ's mass I drink red wine.

ANONYMOUS

✠

THE SPRING PILGRIMAGE

IN SPRING-TIME, PILGRIMS FLOCK TO CANTERBURY TO VISIT THE SHRINE OF THOMAS À BECKET

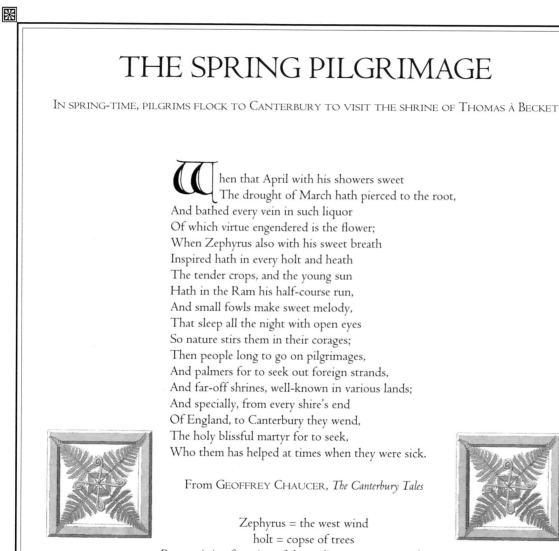

When that April with his showers sweet
The drought of March hath pierced to the root,
And bathed every vein in such liquor
Of which virtue engendered is the flower;
When Zephyrus also with his sweet breath
Inspired hath in every holt and heath
The tender crops, and the young sun
Hath in the Ram his half-course run,
And small fowls make sweet melody,
That sleep all the night with open eyes
So nature stirs them in their corages;
Then people long to go on pilgrimages,
And palmers for to seek out foreign strands,
And far-off shrines, well-known in various lands;
And specially, from every shire's end
Of England, to Canterbury they wend,
The holy blissful martyr for to seek,
Who them has helped at times when they were sick.

From GEOFFREY CHAUCER, *The Canterbury Tales*

Zephyrus = the west wind
holt = copse of trees
Ram = Aries, first sign of the zodiac   corages = hearts
palmers = pilgrims who carried a palm-leaf to show they had been to the Holy Land

A RIDING PARTY, from *The Collected Works of Christine de Pisan*, The Master of the Cité des Dames

Marvellous Tales

Let Each Person Choose
Whatever Subject they Fancy Most

STAG HUNTING, from Gaston Phebus's *Livre de la Chasse*

LET US TELL STORIES

It was no sooner three in the afternoon than the queen arose and ordered all the company to be called, saying that too much sleep in the daytime was unwholesome; and they went into a meadow of deep grass where the sun had little force. Having the benefit of a pleasant breeze, they sat down in a circle as the queen had commanded, and she spoke as follows:

'As the sun has risen rather high, and the heat grows excessive, and nothing is to be heard but the chirping of the grasshoppers among the olives, it would be madness for us to think of moving for a while. This is an airy place, and here are chessboards and gammon-tables to amuse yourselves with, but if you are ruled by me, you will not play at all, since that often makes one party uneasy without any great pleasure to the other player or the onlooker.

'Instead, let us begin by telling stories, and in this way one person will entertain the whole company. By the time each of us has told a tale, the worst part of the day will be over, and then we can amuse ourselves as we like best. If this is agreeable to you, then (for I wait to know what you would prefer) let us begin; if not, you are free to follow your own desires until the evening.'

This proposal was approved by everybody, and the queen continued, 'Let each person for this first day choose whatever subject they fancy most.'

From GIOVANNI BOCCACCIO, *The Decameron*

COURTLY FIGURES IN THE CASTLE GROUNDS, April scene from *Les Très Riches Heures du Duc de Berry*, The Limbourg Brothers

ST CHRISTOPHER, French Book of Hours by the Fastolf Master

ST CHRISTOPHER'S BURDEN

One time, as he slept in his lodge, he heard the voice of a child who called him and said: 'Christopher, come out and carry me over the river.' Then he awoke and went out, but he found no one. And when he was again in his house, he heard the same voice and he ran out and found nobody. The third time he was called and came thither, and found a child beside the river bank, who asked him courteously to bear him over the water.

And then Christopher lifted up the child on his shoulders, and took his staff, and entered the river in order to cross it. And the water of the river arose and swelled more and more: and the child was as heavy as lead, and always as he went farther the water increased and grew more, and the child became heavier and heavier, insomuch that Christopher felt great anguish and was afraid that he would be drowned. And when he had escaped with great pain, and had crossed the water, and set the child aground, he said to the child: 'Child, thou hast put me in great peril; thou weighest almost as if, had I all the world upon me, I might bear no greater burden.' And the child answered: 'Christopher, marvel thee nothing, for thou hast not only borne all the world upon thee, but thou hast borne upon thy shoulders He that created and made all the world. I am Jesu Christ the King, whom thou servest in this work. And because thou know what I say to be the truth, set thy staff in the earth by thy house, and thou shalt see tomorrow that it shall bear flowers and fruit,' and anon he vanished from his eyes.

And then Christopher set his staff in the earth, and when he arose the next morning, he found his staff like a palmier bearing flowers, leaves and dates.

From JACOBUS DE VORAGINE, *The Golden Legend*

✠

THE WOUNDED HIND

In the thickest part of a dense bush, he saw a snow-white hind, with a stag's antlers on her head, couched with her faun. When she heard the hound bark, the hind gave a great leap, and Guigemar took up his bow and shot her, wounding her just above the hoof. At once she dropped to the ground. The arrow, however, was deflected back at Guigemar, piercing him in the thigh and then driving through to his horse, so that he was forced to dismount, and collapsed on to the thick grass next to the stricken hind. The wounded animal, writhing with pain, cried out against him: 'Hear, wretch! I am wounded to death, and you, vile creature, who have destroyed me, may your fate be this: may you never find any cure for your hurt! May neither herb nor root, physician nor potion ever cure the gash in your thigh, until a woman heals you who will suffer as great pain and grief for love of you as ever woman was forced to endure, and you in your turn will suffer so much because of her that all those who have loved since time began will be astonished. And now, go away! Leave me in peace!'

From MARIE DE FRANCE, 'Guigemar'

✠

THE WILTON DIPTYCH (reverse right-hand panel), French (?) School

THE GATHERING BEFORE THE STAG HUNT, from Gaston Phebus's *Livre de la Chasse*

UP BEFORE DAWN

Very early, before daylight, the company rose from their beds. Those guests who were keen to leave called their grooms, and they made haste to saddle the horses, making ready the tackle and packing the saddle-bags. The nobles prepared to ride out richly equipped; they leapt lightly on to their horses, seizing their bridles. Everyone was content, each in his own fashion. The vigorous lord of that land was not the last to be ready to ride out with a full cohort of men; he ate a hasty snack after hearing mass, and then hurried with his bugle to the hunting-field. By the time the first shafts of daylight gleamed on earth, he and his men were on their horses. Then the expert huntsmen leashed their hounds in pairs, unfastened the kennel doors and summoned them out with three single notes on the horn, lustily blown. The hounds bayed at the sound and made a great commotion; those that rushed after false scents were punished and sent back by a hundred huntsmen, so my information goes, each one of the best. The hounds' keepers took up their positions, and the huntsmen unleashed the hounds. The clear tones of the horn set the forest in a clamour.

From ANONYMOUS, *Sir Gawayn and the Grene Knyght*

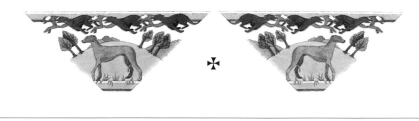

THE MAIDEN IN THE MOOR LAY

The maiden in the moor lay,
In the moor lay;
Seven full nights,
Seven full nights,
The maiden in the moor lay,
In the moor lay,
Seven full nights and a day.

Well was her food.
What was her food?
The primrose and the –
The primrose and the –
Well was her food.
What was her food?
The primrose and the violet.

Well was her drink.
What was her drink?
The cold water of the –
The cold water of the –
Well was her drink.
What was her drink?
The cold water of the well-spring.

Well was her bower.
What was her bower?
The red rose and the –
The red rose and the –
Well was her bower.
What was her bower?
The red rose and the lily flower.

ANONYMOUS

MARY MAGDALEN, Rogier van der Weyden

EMILIA IN HER GARDEN, Hours of the Duke of Burgundy

LOVE STRIKES THE PRISONER PALAMON

The great tower, that was so immensely strong,
And in the castle was the chief dungeon,
Where these two knights were held in prison,
As I have told you and shall tell you more,
Closely adjoined to the same garden wall
Where Emily wandered, the fresh May enjoying.
Bright was the sun, and very clear that morning,
And Palamon, the unhappy prisoner,
As was his custom, by leave of his jailer,
Had risen, and was idling in a chamber high,
From which the noble city he could spy,
And also the garden with its branches green,
Where the bright Emily could now be seen
Walking about, and strolling up and down.
This sorrowful prisoner, this Palamon,
Pent in his chamber, pacing to and fro,
Was grumbling to himself of all his woe,
Regretting he was born, and oft he said, 'Alas,'
And so it happened, by some extraordinary pass,
That through the window, thick with many a bar
Of hefty iron, like a solid wooden spar,
He cast his eyes on fair Emilia,
And cried out a most heartfelt, 'Ah!',
As though he had been stung right to the heart,
And at that cry Arcite at once did start
And said, 'Dear cousin, what on earth can ail thee,
You're deathly pale, a horrid sight to see!'

From GEOFFREY CHAUCER, 'The Knight's Tale'

GATHOLONABES' EARTHLY PARADISE

ON THE ISLAND OF MILSTORAK, THE WILY GATHOLONABES CONSTRUCTS AN EARTHLY PARADISE, WITH ALL MANNER OF FRUITS AND FLOWERS AND EXOTIC BEASTS, AND PEOPLED WITH BEAUTIFUL MAIDENS . . .

And when any good knight, who was hardy and noble, came to see this royalty, he would lead him into his paradise, and show him these wonderful things for his enjoyment, and the marvellous and delicious song of various birds, and the beautiful damsels, and the fair wells of milk, of wine and of honey, plenteously running. And he would arrange for a variety of musical instruments to sound in a high tower, so merrily that it was a joy to hear, and no man saw the craft that lay behind this. And those, he said, were angels of God, and that place was Paradise, that God had promised to his friends, saying, '*Dabo vobis terram fluentem lacte et melle.*' And then he would make them drink a special drink, which would quickly make them drunk; and they would take even greater delight than they had before. And then he would say to them that if they would die for him and for his love, that after their death they should come to his paradise; and they should be of the same age as those damsels, and they should play with them, and still they would be maidens. And after that he would put them into a yet fairer paradise, where they should see God with their own eyes, in His majesty and His bliss. And then he would reveal to them his intention, and tell them that if they would go slay such a lord or such a man, who was his enemy or who opposed his wishes, that they should not fear to do it and to be slain for it themselves. For after their death, he would put them into another paradise, that was a hundred-fold more beautiful than anything in the previous one; and there they should dwell with the fairest damsels in existence, and play with them for ever more.

And thus many vigorous young men went to slay great lords who were his enemies in various countries, and got themselves killed, in hope of having that paradise.

From *The Travels of Sir John Mandeville*

✠

Dabo vobis terram fluentem lacte et melle = I shall give you a land flowing with milk and honey

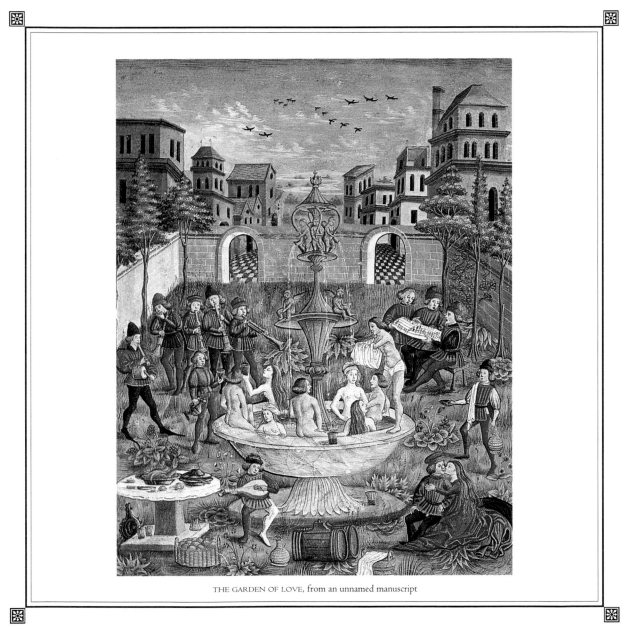

THE GARDEN OF LOVE, from an unnamed manuscript

ENTRY OF YOUNG LOUIS II OF ANJOU INTO PARIS, Froissart's *Chronicle*

THE FAIR MAID OF ASTOLAT

By chance King Arthur and Queen Guenever were speaking together at a window, and as they looked towards the Thames, they espied the black barge, and marvelled what it might mean. Then the King called Sir Kay, and showed him it . . . 'Go you thither,' said the King unto Sir Kay, 'and take with you Sir Brandiles and Sir Agravaine, and bring me ready word what is there.' Then these three knights departed, and came to the barge, and went in; and there they found the fairest corpse lying in a rich bed that ever they saw, and a poor man sitting at the end of the barge, and no word would he speak.

So these three knights returned to the King again, and told him what they had found. 'That fair corpse will I see,' said King Arthur. And then the King took the Queen by the hand and went thither. The King ordered the barge to be secured, and the King and the Queen went in, with certain knights with them, and there they saw a fair gentlewoman lying in a rich bed, covered to her waist with many rich clothes, and all was of cloth of gold; and she lay as though she had smiled. The Queen espied the letter in her right hand, and told the King thereof. The King took it in his hand, and said, 'Now I am sure this letter will tell what she was, and why she is come hither.' The King and Queen went out of the barge; and . . . when the King was come within his chamber, he called many knights about him, and said that he would know openly what was written within that letter. The King broke it open, and made a clerk read it out. And this was the content of the letter:

'Most noble knight, my lord Sir Launcelot du Lake, now hath death made us two at debate for your love; I was your lover, that men called the fair maiden of Astolat, therefore unto all ladies I make my complaint, that ye will pray for my soul, and bury me at the least, and offer ye my mass-penny. This is my last request, and a pure maid I died, I take God to my witness. Pray for my soul, Sir Launcelot, as thou art a knight peerless.'

This was all the substance of the letter. And when it was read, the Queen and all the knights wept for pity of the doleful complaints.

From SIR THOMAS MALORY, *Le Morte D'Arthur*

WHEN NETTLES IN WINTER
BRING FORTH ROSES RED

When nettles in winter bring forth roses red,
   And all manner of thorns bear figs naturally,
And brooms bear apples in every mead,
And laurels bear spikes abundantly,
And oaks bear dates so plenteously,
And leeks give honey in superfluence –
Then put in a woman your trust and confidence.

When sparrows build churches and steeples high,
And wrens carry sacks to the mill,
And curlews carry cloths horses to dry,
And sea-mews bring butter to the market to sell,
And wood-doves wear wood-knives thieves to kill,
And vultures to goslings show obedience –
Then put in a woman your trust and confidence.

When crabs take woodcocks in forests and parks,
And hares are lured by the sweetness of snails,
And camels with their hair take swallows and perch,
And mice mow corn by waving of their tails,
When ducks on the dunghill seek Christ's Blood at Hailes,
When shrews to their husbands give no offence –
Then put in a woman your trust and confidence.   ANONYMOUS

wood-knives = hunting knives
Hailes = the blood of Christ was kept as a precious relic at Hailes Abbey in Gloucestershire

106

JUNO IN A CHARIOT DRAWN BY PEACOCKS, from Giovanni Boccaccio's *Filocolo*

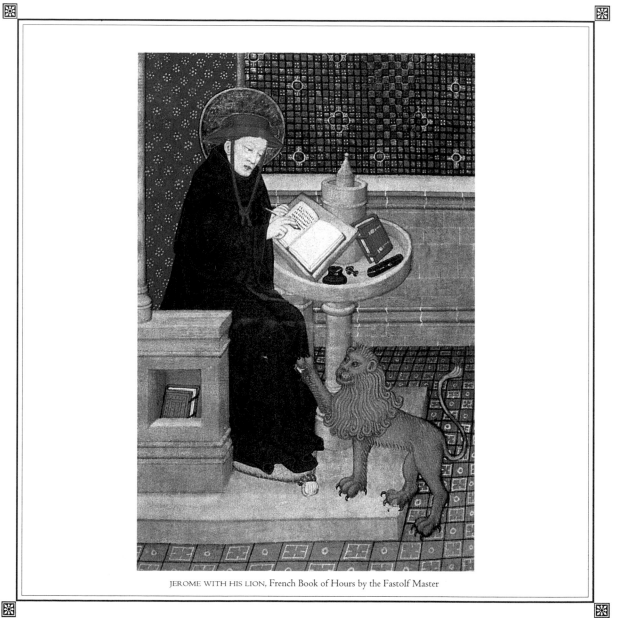

JEROME WITH HIS LION, French Book of Hours by the Fastolf Master

JEROME AND THE LION

One day towards evening, as Jerome sat with his brethren listening to the holy lesson, suddenly a lion came limping into the monastery. When the brethren saw him, at once they fled, but Jerome went towards the lion as he would approach a guest, and then the lion showed him his foot, which was hurt. Then Jerome called his brethren and commanded them to wash the lion's feet and carefully to seek out and search for the wound. That done, they found that the pad of the lion's foot was sorely hurt and pricked with a thorn. Then this holy man set himself diligently to cure the foot and healed him, and the lion abode ever after as a tame beast with them.

From JACOBUS DE VORAGINE, *The Golden Legend*

✛

SETH AND THE OIL OF MERCY

And the Christian men, that dwell beyond the sea in Greece, say that the tree of the cross, that we call cypress, came from that tree that Adam ate the apple off; and that find they written. And they say also, that their scripture saith, that Adam was sick, and said to his son Seth that he should go to the angel that kept Paradise, that he would send him oil of mercy, with which to anoint his body so that he might have health. And Seth went. But the angel would not let him come in, and said to him, that he might not have the oil of mercy. But he took him three seeds of the same tree that his father ate the apple off; and told him, as soon as his father was dead, that he should put these three seeds under his tongue, and bury him so . . . And when Seth came again, he found his father near death. And when he was dead, he did with the seeds as the angel had told him; from which sprang three trees, from which the cross was made that bore good fruit and blessed, our Lord Jesu Christ; through whom, Adam and all that come of him should be saved and delivered from fear of death without end, unless it be by their own default.

From *The Travels of Sir John Mandeville*

THE CRUCIFIED CHRIST WITH THE VIRGIN MARY, SAINTS AND ANGELS, Raphael

THE BATTLE BETWEEN KING ARTHUR AND MORDRED, St Alban's *Chronicle*

A BATTLE BETWEEN TWO NOBLE KNIGHTS

T hen Sir Launcelot spoke to King Arthur, who was above him on the tower, and said, 'My lord and noble king who made me a knight, . . . I must needs defend myself, since Sir Gawaine has accused me of treason. It is greatly against my will to fight against anyone of your high blood, but now I cannot escape it, I am driven to it like a beast at bay.'

At this, Sir Gawaine said to Sir Launcelot, 'Sir Launcelot, if you dare to do battle, leave your babbling and come on, and let us ease our hearts.' And so Sir Launcelot began to arm himself, and mounted his horse, and each of the knights had great spears in their hands, and the multitude outside still stood apart. And the noble knights came out of the city in great numbers, so many that when King Arthur saw the throng of men and knights, he was amazed, and said to himself, 'Alas, that ever Sir Launcelot was against me, for now I see he has been forbearing with me.' Thus the agreement was made that no man should come near the opponents, or interfere with them, until one of them were dead or had yielded.

Then Sir Gawaine and Sir Launcelot set a great distance between them and they came together with all the power of which their horses were capable, as fast as they could gallop, and each smote the other in the midst of his shield. But the knights were so strong and their spears so immense, that their horses could not endure the impact of their blows, and they fell to the ground. So they left their horses and held up their shields to defend themselves; then they stood face to face, and struck many harsh blows, one to the other, so that the blood flowed freely from many wounds.

Thus Sir Launcelot fought with Sir Gawaine . . .

From Sir Thomas Malory, *Le Morte D'Arthur*

✠

THE ILLUSTRATIONS

The illustrations in *Through the Glass Window Shines the Sun* include illuminations from some of the great decorative manuscripts of the late Middle Ages, and paintings by medieval and early Renaissance masters.

Many of the illuminations are taken from Books of Hours. Generally intended for private worship and owned by wealthy collectors and patrons, these often highly ornamental manuscripts contain sets of prayers designated by the church for use at certain hours of the day. The decorative possibilities of these texts were first developed in the thirteenth century, and culminated in the particularly grand and beautiful Books of Hours of the fourteenth and fifteenth centuries.

As with paintings of the period, the scenes were generally religious, commonly depicting the Life of the Virgin, Christ's Passion, and the lives and deaths of saints. The calendar decorations, however, were often secular, showing the occupations traditionally associated with a particular month. Because of this, non-religious themes, including the exploration of landscape, can be found in manuscript illuminations some time before they were considered appropriate subject matter for larger-scale paintings.

One of the most impressive Books of Hours is the *Très Riches Heures* commissioned by the French patron and collector, Jean, Duc de Berry, from the three Limbourg brothers, and executed between 1413 and 1416. The three images selected for this anthology are the January, April and May calendar illuminations. Distinguished by

their luminous use of colour and particularly skilled draftsmanship and composition, they communicate the elegance and wealth of court life along with a strong feeling for the beauty of the countryside. In each illustration, attention is focused on the elegant and stylized figures in the foreground.

The calendar miniatures of the Flemish artist Simon Bening, dating from around 1540, show a very different balance between figures and landscape. In his October scene, page 84, the agricultural workers and their activities are less important than the scenery, and the eye travels back from the ploughed field in the foreground with its buzz of activity, to the road with tiny horsemen, while a distant church spire indicates a village hidden among the trees.

The Bedford Hours, dating from between 1414 and 1423, belonged to John of Lancaster, Duke of Bedford. On page 24, we see the Duke himself, kneeling before St George, patron of England and of the Order of the Garter, whose ermine-lined robe the saint wears. In 'The Exit from the Arc', page 32, the artist has used this popular story to demonstrate his pictorial and compositional skills. As the animals emerge on to a scene of watery devastation, under the watchful eye of Mrs Noah, her husband gets rollicking drunk, a later episode in the biblical narrative, while at the bottom left of the picture, a pair of legs pokes dejectedly out of the waves, and a camel sets off along a shore littered with bones.

In a rather different style are the beautiful Italian Sforza Hours, commissioned by Bona Sforza, mother of the Duke of Milan. 'The Payment of Judas', page 80, was executed by the artist Giovan Pietro Birago, the leading miniaturist at the Sforza court from around 1490. The bright colours, curly hair and anachronistic costumes are typical of this artist.

Not all manuscripts were religious. The Harley *Roman de la Rose*, Flemish in origin and dating from around 1490–1500, is a brilliantly illuminated edition of this hugely popular French poem. The images reproduced here illustrate stages in the Lover's quest for the Rose, the symbol of romantic love. On page 47, he is seen simultaneously sleeping, getting dressed and setting out for a walk on a fine May morning. Page 70 shows the Lover outside a garden, and on page 53, he joins the dance which is led by Sir Mirth and his lady Gladness.

Apart from portraits, the paintings in this anthology are predominantly religious in subject-matter. Originally part of an altarpiece, 'The Magdalen Reading' (cover) is by the outstanding Netherlandish painter Rogier van der Weyden, and dates from around 1440–50. As in the second painting of the Magdalen by the same artist, on page 99, she is often identified by her jar of ointment, with which she anointed Christ's feet, and her costly dress.

Saints were popular subjects, allowing the artist both to tell a story and to display his skill in depicting the human form. The meeting of St Joachim and St Anne, page 45, by the Master of Moulins (Jean Hey), celebrates the greeting of the parents of the Virgin, said to have taken place at the Golden Gate of Jerusalem, seen here as the entrance to a typical medieval walled city. St Dorothy, page 31, was mocked on the way to her execution by a lawyer who asked her to send him roses and apples from the Garden of Paradise. She, of course,

obliged, and the lawyer was converted and martyred in his turn. Her basket of flowers includes the legendary roses. In Raphael's fine painting, page 69, St Catherine is shown with the wheel on which she was tortured for refusing to abandon her Christian beliefs. On pages 12/13, she appears again in the altarpiece by Gerard David, painted around 1509, which celebrates the mystic marriage of Catherine with Christ: the baby holds a ring ready to place on her finger. Also in the scene is Mary Magdalen with her ointment jar, St Barbara, and the patron who has donated the painting to the church (probably St Donatian's at Bruges). They are grouped around the Virgin and Christ Child, whose miraculous birth is celebrated in 'The Annunciation' (page 23) and 'The Adoration of the Kings' (title page), both by a Follower of the Italian painter Fra Angelico.

Christ's Passion offered possibilities both for dramatic narrative, and for exploring intense feeling. In Pieter Brueghel the Elder's 'Procession to Calvary', pages 62/3, the central stories, Christ staggering under the weight of the cross and the grief of the Virgin, are almost swallowed up in the great press of folk swarming up the hill to Calvary. In 'Christ Mocked', page 35, Hieronymus Bosch indicates Christ's gentleness and passivity by his mild expression and pallor, in contrast to the more colourful brutality of his tormentors. The bully, top right, wears the spiked collar of a ferocious dog. Raphael's formal and almost decorative image of the crucified Christ, page 111, minimizes pain and torment to provide a focus for devout contemplation. The Virgin (left) is reflective rather than anguished, and she and St John look out of the picture, inviting the beholder to brood on the meaning of Christ's sacrifice.

THE WRITERS

*Texts have been edited from manuscripts or early editions,
and carefully modernized. BL = British Library;
Bod = Bodleian Library, Oxford.*

ANONYMOUS: many of the poems in this anthology appear anonymously in the manuscript collections listed below.

'A Friendship Lost': a visual game with a serious message. BL: Harley 116, f.170b.

'A God and Yet a Man': a meditation on the paradox of Christ's combined humanity and divinity. Bod: Rawlinson B. 332 (11670).

'A Precious Pearl': a small section from the late-fourteenth-century alliterative poem, *Pearl*, in which a bereaved man dreams of a pearl-maiden, who schools him in understanding and acceptance of his loss. BL: MS Facs 998 (Cotton Nero, A.x.).

'A Song for St George': St George was the patron saint of England. BL: Egerton 3307, f.63b.

'Adam Lay Y-bounden': BL: Sloane 2593, f.11.

'Bring Us in Good Ale': abridged. Bod: Eng. poet. e.I (29734), f.41b.

'By This Fire I Warm My Hands': Bod: MS. Digby 88, f.97v.

'Deo Gracias, Anglia': celebrates the victory of Henry V at Agincourt in 1415. Bod: Arch. Selden B.26 (3340), f.17b.

'I Have a Young Sister': a riddle poem. BL: Sloane 2593, f.11a.

'I Must Go Walk the Wood So Wild': Hunt. EL 1160, f.11b.

'I Sing of a Maiden': celebrates the Incarnation of Christ, the moment of conception when the angel spoke. BL: Sloane 2593, f.10b.

'In a Glorious Garden Green': a part-song for three voices. BL: Add. 5465, f.108b.

'Noel, Noel, Noel': Bod: Eng. poet. e.I (29734), f.47b.

'Of All Creatures Women be Best': abridged. Bod: Eng. poet. e.I (29734), f.55b.

'She Saw Me in Church': Bod: Lat. misc. c.66, f.94a.

'The Bride's Song': a section of a longer song. BL: Harley 7578, f.110.

'The Corpus Christi Carol': Balliol College, Oxford: 354, f.165b.

'The Maiden in the Moor Lay': expanded from the original, which appears, much abbreviated, on a battered scrap of manuscript. Bod: Rawlinson D.913 (13679), f.1b.

'Up Before Dawn': from the late-fourteenth-century alliterative poem, *Sir Gawayn and the Grene Knyght*.

'Western Wind': the speaker, becalmed at sea, prays for the trade winds. BL: Royal Appendix 58, f.5a.

'When Nettles in Winter Bring Forth Roses Red': abridged. Bod: Eng. poet. e.1 (29734), f.44a.

GIOVANNI BOCCACCIO (1313–75), son of a Florentine merchant, writer and humanist, a Dante enthusiast and friend of Petrarch. *The Decameron* is a collection of a hundred stories culled from many sources and put together between 1349 and 1351. As the result of a plague, a group of Florentines move to the countryside where they amuse themselves by telling stories. 'Let Us Tell Stories': adapted from the translation by Charles Balguy, London 1741.

MARGERY BREWS (?–*c*.1495) daughter of Sir Thomas Brews of Topcroft, Norfolk. Despite the difficulties over money referred to in 'A Valentine Letter', she married John Paston in 1477, a love match encouraged by her mother. The Paston Letters, dating from 1425 to the early sixteenth century, are a substantial collection of correspondence between members of this family of Norfolk landowners. BL: Add. 43490, f.23a.

CHARLES OF ORLEANS (1391–1465) French nobleman, poet and soldier. He was taken prisoner at Agincourt in 1415, and remained a prisoner in England until he was ransomed in 1440, using the time to compose graceful and musical ballads, rondels, etc, in French and English. 'A Confession' was very probably his composition. BL: Harley 682, f.88b.

GEOFFREY CHAUCER (*c*.1343–1400), poet, was employed for most of his life at the English court. He began *The Canterbury Tales* in *c*. 1387, but this ambitious project was never completed. The twenty-four tales that survive were developed from a wide variety of sources. 'The Spring Pilgrimage', from the General Prologue, sets the scene for the pilgrims' journey. 'A May Dance' and 'Love Strikes the Prisoner Palamon' describe crucial encounters in two of the most popular tales.

WILLIAM DUNBAR (?1465–?1513) Scottish poet and priest, is perhaps best known for his elegy, 'Lament for the Makers', which reflects on the transitoriness of life and fame. He probably died at the Battle of Flodden, where the Earl of Surrey, on behalf of Henry VIII, defeated James IV of Scotland. 'To a Ladye' plays on the double meaning of the word 'rue'.

HENRY VIII (1491–1547) King of England (from 1509), husband, accomplished poet and musician. 'Green Groweth the Holly' is headed 'The kyng h. viii' and accompanied with music for three voices. BL: Add. 31922, f.37b.

HENRY HOWARD, EARL OF SURREY (c.1517–47) was, with his near contemporary Sir Thomas Wyatt, a significant innovator in English poetry. Spanning the late medieval and early Renaissance periods, he developed the sonnet form, adapting it from Italian models to suit the rhymes and rhythms of the English language. 'So Cruel Prison', abridged from a longer poem, records his unhappy imprisonment in Windsor. 'The Means to Attain Happy Life' is based on an epigram by the Roman poet, Martial.

JACOBUS DE VORAGINE (1230–98), an Italian Dominican friar, archbishop of Genoa. His *Legenda Aurea* (*The Golden Legend*), a hugely popular compilation in Latin of saints' lives, was published in English by William Caxton in 1483. 'Ave Maria', 'Jerome and the Lion' and 'St Christopher's Burden' are based on Caxton's version.

JULIAN OF NORWICH (c.1342–after 1416), recluse and mystic, lived in a cell at St Julian's Church, Norwich. Her *Revelations of Divine Love*, probably written after 1393, describe visions experienced during an illness many years previously, and her meditations on what was revealed to her. 'All Manner of Things Shall be Well': BL: Sloane 2499, f.41.

MARGERY KEMPE (c.1373–c.1439), mystic and traveller, persuaded her husband to allow her to lead a celibate life so that she could pursue God with dedication. An enthusiastic pilgrim, she described her adventures in her autobiography, *The Book of Margery Kempe*. 'Margery Kempe Hazards the Dangerous Voyage Across the Sea' from BL: Add. 61823, f.49.

GUILLAUME DE LORRIS (d. 1237) wrote the first 4,058 lines of the French allegorical romance, *Roman de la Rose*, which numbers around 22,000 words in total. De Lorris's section reflects the courtly love ethic that was current at the time: the Lover sets out to find the Rose, symbol of his Lady's love, encountering various allegorical figures on the way. 'A Fruitful Garden': from Geoffrey Chaucer's translation, *The Romaunt of the Rose*.

The identity of SIR THOMAS MALORY (d. 1471) has not been clearly established, although he is thought to have been Sir Thomas Malory of Newbold Revell in Warwickshire, who was imprisoned for rape and theft after 1450. 'A Battle Between Two Noble Knights', 'The Fair Maid of Astolat' and 'The Love Potion': from *Le Morte D'Arthur*, a series of narratives about the legendary King Arthur and his knights.

The biography of SIR JOHN MANDEVILLE is even more obscure. His *Travels* first appeared in Anglo-Norman French in 1356 and were soon widely translated. The text, culled from diverse sources, entertainingly tours the Holy Land and the Near East, combining geographic and natural lore with marvels and popular fables. See 'Gatholonabes' Earthly Paradise' and 'Seth and the Oil of Mercy'. BL: Cotton Titus c.XVI.

Little is known about the French poet MARIE DE FRANCE. The *Lais* (Lays) and *Fables* attributed to her were probably written during the latter part of the twelfth century, and she appears to have had knowledge of court life and to have lived for a time in England. 'The Wounded Hind' is from the lay 'Guigemar', a romantic tale in which a young man and woman remain faithful to one another despite numerous setbacks and obstacles. Translated from Anglo-Norman. BL: Harley 978.

JAMES RYMAN was probably a friar at a Franciscan convent in Canterbury. 'A Christmas Carol' (*c.* 1492?) is from a manuscript collection of his Carols in praise of the Virgin. Abridged. Cambridge University Library: Ee. I, 12, ff.34r–34v.

JOHN SKELTON (?1460–1529), poet and churchman, was tutor to Prince Henry (later Henry VIII), and later became Rector of Diss in Norfolk. 'To Mistress Margaret Hussey' is one of his most charming pieces, as fresh and vivid as the woman it describes.

SIR THOMAS WYATT (1503–42) served as a diplomat under Henry VIII. Through his experiments with metre and diction he encouraged the development of English poetry, and, like his near contemporary Surrey, laid the foundations for the work of the great Elizabethan poets. 'The Perils of Diplomacy' is a powerful reworking of a sonnet by the Italian poet Petrarch, often a starting-off point for Wyatt. Much lighter in tone is the courtly 'The Stolen Kiss'.

✠

EDITOR'S ACKNOWLEDGEMENTS

The editor would like to thank The Master and Fellows of Balliol College, Oxford; the British Library; the Bodleian Library, Oxford; and The Syndics of Cambridge University Library for permission to use manuscripts from their collections (see The Writers for full manuscript details). The staff of these libraries gave graciously of their time, as did Stephanie Watson of The Bridgeman Art Library, Alessandra Pinzani of SCALA, and Maureen Pemberton of the Bodleian Library Picture Research Department. The excellent *Giotto to Dürer*, by Jill Dunkerton, Susan Foister, Dillian Gordon and Nicholas Penny (New Haven & London, 1991), was a useful guide to early Renaissance paintings in the National Gallery collection. Vivien Bowler and Mari Roberts at Little, Brown provided welcome support and expertise, and David Fordham and Nadine Wickenden made their customary invaluable contributions to the appearance of the book. To all, many thanks.

PICTURE ACKNOWLEDGEMENTS

The publisher would like to thank the following museums and galleries for supplying illustrations:

BODLEIAN LIBRARY, OXFORD: p.57 Ms Auct D inf 2.11 f.59v Noah's Ark, French Book of Hours by the Fastolf Master, mid-15th century; p.58 Ms Laud Misc 751, f.32r Two seated figures with empty chessboard, from a French translation of Quintus Curtius, *Historia Alexandri Magni*, anonymous Flemish artist, *c.* 1470–80; p.76 MS Auct D inf 2.11, f.44v St George, French Book of Hours by the Fastolf Master, mid-15th century; p.92 Ms Auct D inf 2.11 f.48v St Christopher, French Book of Hours by the Fastolf Master, mid-15th century; p.107 MS Canon Ital 85 f.1 Juno, anonymous Italian artist, from Giovanni Boccaccio, *Filocolo*, a copy made for Ludovico III Gonzaga, Duke of Mantua; p.108 Ms Auct D inf 2.11 f.231v St Jerome, French Book of Hours by the Fastolf Master, mid-15th century.

BRIDGEMAN ART LIBRARY, LONDON: p.16 St Barbara from the right wing of the Werl Altarpiece (detail), 1438 (panel), Master of Flemalle (R. Campin) 1375/8–1444 (attr) (Prado, Madrid); p.19 The Descent from the Cross, Rogier van der Weyden 1399–1464 (Prado, Madrid); p.20 Cott Aug A V f.345v Flemish landscape with a watermill in the foreground and a windmill in the background, *Histoire Universelle*, attrib. Marmion (British Library, London); p.28 Ms 2 f.65v The visitation, The Hours of Marshal Jean de Boucicaut (Use of Paris), Boucicaut Hours, early 15th century (Musée Jacquemart-Andre, Paris); p.39 Adam and Eve in the Garden of Eden, Lucas Cranach the Elder 1472–1553 (Kunsthistorisches Museum, Vienna); p.50 Roy 2 A XVI f.3 Henry VIII seated, reading in a bedroom with Latin marginal notes in Henry VIII's hand by John Mallard, Henry VIII psalter, *c.* 1540; p.53 Harl 4425 f.14v–15 Gladness leads the dance: the Lover and his Rose, illuminated by the Master of the Prayer Books of *c.* 1500, Bruges, *Roman de la Rose, c.* 1487–95 (British Library, London); p.61 Ms 65/1284 f.5v May: courtly figures on horseback by the Limbourg brothers, *Les Très Riches Heures du Duc de Berry*, early 15th century (Musée Conde, Chantilly/Giraudon); p.63 The Procession to Calvary, Pieter Brueghel the Elder *c.* 1515–69 (Kunsthistorisches Museum, Vienna); p.66 Ms 65/1284 f.1v January: banquet scene by the Limbourg brothers, *Les Très Riches Heures du Duc de Berry*, early 15th century (Musée Conde, Chantilly/Giraudon); p.70 Harl 4425 f.12v Garden scene, the Lover and Dame Oyeuse without, illuminated by the Master of the Prayer Books of *c.* 1500, Bruges, *Roman de la Rose, c.* 1487–95 (British Library, London); p.74 George Grisze, Hans Holbein 1497/8–1543 (Staatliche Gemäldegalerie, Berlin); p.79 Roy 16 G V f.56 Gaia Caecilia or Tanaquil, with loom and women spinning, from 'De Claris Mulieribus', *Works of Giovanni Boccaccio*, 1313–75 (British Library, London); p.83 Add 19720 f.117v An orchard with people picking fruit, French, Croissen's *Manual of Agriculture*, late 15th century (British Library, London); p.84 Add 18855 October: ploughing and sowing, Book of Hours, *c.* 1540, Simon Bening 1483–1561 (Victoria and Albert Museum, London); p.89 Stag hunting, Gaston Phebus, from *Livre de la Chasse*, begun 1387 (Bibliothèque Nationale, Paris); p.91 Ms 65/1284 f.4v April: courtly figures in the castle grounds by the Limbourg brothers, *Les Très Riches Heures du Duc de Berry*, early 15th century (Musée Conde, Chantilly/Giraudon); p.96 The gathering before the stag hunt, from Gaston Phebus's 'Count of Foix and Bearn 1331–1391' Book of Hunting, *Livre de la Chasse*, begun 1387 (Bibliothèque Nationale, Paris); p.99 Mary Magdalen, Rogier van der Weyden 1399–1464 (Louvre, Paris); p.100 120.482 Emilia in her garden, Hours of the Duke of Burgundy, 1454–55 (Bibliothek National, Vienna); p.104 Fr 2645 f.321v Entry of young Louis II of Anjou into Paris, Froissart's *Chronicle*, late 15th century (Bibliothèque Nationale, Paris); p.112 Ms 6 f.66v Battle between King Arthur and Mordred, English, with Flemish illuminations, St Alban's *Chronicle*, late 15th century (Lambeth Palace Library, London).

BRITISH LIBRARY By permission of the British Library: p.24 Add Ms 18850 f.256b John, Duke of Bedford, at Prayer before St George, The Bedford Hours, The Master of the Munich Golden Legend; p.32 Add Ms 18850 f.16b The Exit from the Ark, The Bedford Hours, The Master of the Munich Golden Legend; p.36 Egerton Ms 1070 f.32v Apparition of the Angels to the Shepherds, The Book of Hours of René Anjou, The Egerton Master; p.42 Add Ms 24098 f.21b April: Lovers in a Garden, Flemish calendar, early 16th century; p.47 Harl Ms 4425 f.7 The Lover Asleep, Rising, and Going for a Walk, illuminated by the Master of the Prayer Books of *c.* 1500, Bruges, *Roman de la Rose, c.* 1487–95; p.48 Harl Ms 4431 f.4 Christine de Pisan, Writing, *Collected Works of Christine de Pisan*, The Master of the Cité des Dames; p.65 BL Roy Ms 16 F ii f.73 The Tower of London, manuscript of the poems of Charles of Orleans; p.80 Add Ms 34294 f.137r Payment of Judas, Sforza Hours, Giovan Pietro Birago; p.87 Harl Ms 4431 f.81 A Riding Party, *Collected Works of Christine de Pisan*, The Master of the Cité des Dames.

COURTAULD INSTITUTE GALLERIES, LONDON: p.27 Adam and Eve (detail), Lucas Cranach the Elder (Lee Collection).

NATIONAL GALLERY: cover The Magdalen Reading (detail), Rogier van der Weyden; p.3 The Adoration of the Kings, Follower of Fra Angelico; p.13 The Virgin and Child with Saints and Donor, Gerard David; p.15 The Virgin and Child, Hans Memlinc and Workshop; p.23 Altarpiece: The Annunciation, Follower of Fra Angelico; p.31 St Dorothy (detail), The Master of the Saint Bartholomew Altarpiece; p.35 Christ Mocked (The Crowning with Thorns), Hieronymus Bosch; p.41 Portrait of a Lady, Workshop of Rogier van der Weyden; p.45 Charlemagne and the Meeting of Saints Joachim and Anne, The Master of Moulins (Jean Hey); p.54 Portrait of a Woman of the Hofer Family, unknown Swabian artist; p.69 St Catherine of Alexandria (detail), Raphael; p.95 The Wilton Diptych (reverse right-hand panel), French (?) School; p.111 The Crucified Christ with the Virgin Mary, Saints and Angels, Raphael.

SCALA PHOTO, FLORENCE: p.73 The Capture of Antioch, *Storie degli Imperatori* (Bibliothèque de l'Arsenal, Paris); p.103 The Garden of Love, Ms Lat 209 DX2 14 c. 10r (*il Giardino dell'Amore*, Biblioteca Estense, Modena).